I0620487

To my precious daughters, Joy, Ellie, and Emma:

you are the inspiration behind this book.

Each night, as I pray over your precious lives, I'm reminded of the wonderful gift **God** has given me—the honor of nurturing your hearts, minds, and spirits. May you always look to **Jesus**; may you hear **His** voice in both the quiet moments and the loud; and may you feel **His** loving presence guiding your every step. You are **His** delight and my greatest joy. Keep shining **His** light, my sweet girls, as you walk with **Him** each day and night. I pray that you know, each day of your lives, that you are loved from your head to your toes.

I'll love you forever and ever, no matter what.

For **His** Glory,

Mom

Copyright © 2025 Tricia Patterson
Illustrations © 2025 Anastasia Sivura
Designed by Ryan Webb
Published by Truth at Home Press
Waco, Texas
www.triciapatterson.com

All rights reserved. No part of this publication may be reproduced, stored in a retrieval system, or transmitted in any form or by any means—electronic, mechanical, photocopy, recording, or otherwise—without the prior written permission of the publisher, except in the case of brief quotations used in articles or reviews.

Scripture quotations are from the Holy Bible, New International Version® (NIV®). Copyright © 1973, 1978, 1984, 2011 by Biblica, Inc.™ Used by permission. All rights reserved worldwide.

First Edition
ISBN: 979-8-9992470-0-1 (Hardcover)
ISBN: 979-8-9992470-1-8 (Paperback)

Printed in the United States of America

For permissions, inquiries, or bulk orders, contact:
info@triciapatterson.com

A PRAYER
from Head to Toe

Written by
Tricia Patterson

Illustrated by
Anastasia Sivura

Dear child,

Let's pray from your **head** to your **toes**,
About all the ways **God's** love overflows!
From your head to your feet,
God's love is so sweet!
Let's pray for each part,
And carry **Him** in your heart!

I pray your **mind** will grow to see
How wide and deep **His** love can be.
From sky above to ocean floor,
God's love will hold you forevermore.

I pray your **ears** will hear **God's voice,**
In whispers soft, through quiet and noise.

May you hear **His** Spirit,
soft and true,
And trust all that **He** says about you.

I pray your **eyes** see wonders galore—
In flowers, stars, and oceans' roar!
May you look at others with kindness and grace,
And see **God's** love in every place.
Fix your eyes on **Jesus**, dear,
With **Him**, all things will be clear.

I pray your **nose** will breathe in deep,
The fragrance of **Christ**, so pure and sweet.

May **His** presence fill your every day,
Bringing joy and peace along the way.

I pray your **mouth** will taste and see,
That **God** is good—He's all you need.

Let your lips confess: "**Jesus** is Lord,"
And follow **Him**, now and forevermore.

I pray your **face** beams with **His** light,
Like **God's** own smile, shining bright.
May peace and joy glow on your cheeks,
As **His** love guides you through the weeks.
Let your smile reflect **His** grace and love,
As you walk with **Him**, guided from above.

I pray your **neck** stands tall and proud,
Looking up to God, away from the crowd.

And may your shoulders
    not bear too much—
For **Jesus** will help
    when the road feels rough.

I pray your **heart**
desires **Jesus** alone,
For only through **Him**
can you be fully known.
May you love **Him** above
all things on earth,
And find in **Him**
your true
worth.

I pray you **hunger** for **Jesus** each day,
Craving **His** Word in every way.
May **His** love be the feast that fills you whole,
Satisfying the longings of your soul.

I pray your **arms** will hug and hold,

The lonely, the lost, the young and old.

May you comfort others with love so true,

Just like **Jesus** has done for you.

I pray your **hands** will share and give,
Spreading **God's** love as you live.
May you be the hands of **Jesus**, dear,
Helping others far and near.

I pray your **legs** will leap and play,
Following the **Spirit** each joyful day;
On paths of goodness, right and true,
May you follow **Him** in all you do.

Even when the path is dim,
Follow **His** steps, walk with **Him**.

I pray your **knees**
will hit the ground,
Where mercy and grace
are always found.

In joy or sorrow,
big
or
small,

Kneel before **God**,
He hears it all.

I pray your **feet** are quick to go,
Wherever **Jesus** tells you so.

Let your steps bring light and peace,
Sharing **His** love that will never cease.

I pray your **body**, from **head** to **toe**,
Will glorify **God** as you grow.

You're made in **His** image, so wonderfully bright,
A shining star, glowing with **His** light.

From **head** to **toe**, you're **His** delight,
He'll keep you close, day and night.

Where to Find These Promises in God's Word

Mind

Ephesians 3:17-19: "And I pray that you, being rooted and established in love, may have power, together with all the Lord's holy people, to grasp how wide and long and high and deep is the love of Christ, and to know this love that surpasses knowledge—that you may be filled to the measure of all the fullness of God."

Ears

John 10:27: "My sheep listen to my voice; I know them, and they follow me."

1 Kings 19:12: "And after the earthquake came a fire, but the Lord was not in the fire. And after the fire came a gentle whisper."

Eyes

Psalm 19:1: "The heavens declare the glory of God; the skies proclaim the work of his hands."

Matthew 6:22: "The eye is the lamp of the body. If your eyes are healthy, your whole body will be full of light."

Hebrews 12:2: "Fixing our eyes on Jesus, the pioneer and perfecter of faith."

Nose

2 Corinthians 2:15: "For we are to God the pleasing aroma of Christ among those who are being saved and those who are perishing."

Ephesians 5:2: "And walk in the way of love, just as Christ loved us and gave himself up for us as a fragrant offering and sacrifice to God."

Mouth

Psalm 34:8: "Taste and see that the Lord is good; blessed is the one who takes refuge in him."

Romans 10:9: "If you declare with your mouth, 'Jesus is Lord,' and believe in your heart that God raised him from the dead, you will be saved."

Face

Numbers 6:24-26: "The Lord bless you and keep you; the Lord make his face shine on you and be gracious to you; the Lord turn his face toward you and give you peace."

Psalm 34:5: "Those who look to him are radiant; their faces are never covered with shame."

Neck & Shoulders

Proverbs 3:3: "Let love and faithfulness never leave you; bind them around your neck, write them on the tablet of your heart."

Matthew 11:28-30: "Come to me, all you who are weary and burdened, and I will give you rest. Take my yoke upon you and learn from me, for I am gentle and humble in heart, and you will find rest for your souls. For my yoke is easy and my burden is light."

Heart

Matthew 22:37: "Jesus replied: 'Love the Lord your God with all your heart and with all your soul and with all your mind.'"

Psalm 37:4: "Take delight in the Lord, and he will give you the desires of your heart."

Proverbs 4:23: "Above all else, guard your heart, for everything you do flows from it."

Tummy

Matthew 5:6: "Blessed are those who hunger and thirst for righteousness, for they will be filled."

John 6:35: "Then Jesus declared, 'I am the bread of life. Whoever comes to me will never go hungry, and whoever believes in me will never be thirsty.'"

Arms

Proverbs 17:17: "A friend loves at all times, and a brother is born for a time of adversity."

John 13:34: "A new command I give you: Love one another. As I have loved you, so you must love one another."

Proverbs 31:20: "She opens her arms to the poor and extends her hands to the needy."

Hands

1 Peter 4:10: "Each of you should use whatever gift you have received to serve others, as faithful stewards of God's grace in its various forms."

Galatians 5:13: "Serve one another humbly in love."

Legs

Psalm 23:3: "He refreshes my soul. He guides me along the right paths for his name's sake."

Romans 8:14: "For those who are led by the Spirit of God are the children of God."

Psalm 119:105: "Your word is a lamp for my feet, a light on my path."

Knees

Philippians 2:10: "That at the name of Jesus every knee should bow, in heaven and on earth and under the earth."

Ephesians 3:14: "For this reason I kneel before the Father."

Luke 22:41: "He withdrew about a stone's throw beyond them, knelt down and prayed."

Feet

Isaiah 52:7: "How beautiful on the mountains are the feet of those who bring good news, who proclaim peace, who bring good tidings, who proclaim salvation, who say to Zion, 'Your God reigns!'"

Romans 10:15: "And how can anyone preach unless they are sent? As it is written: 'How beautiful are the feet of those who bring good news!'"

Your Whole Body

Psalm 139:14: "I praise you because I am fearfully and wonderfully made; your works are wonderful, I know that full well."

Genesis 1:27: "So God created mankind in his own image, in the image of God he created them; male and female he created them."

Philippians 2:15: "Then you will shine among them like stars in the sky."

www.ingramcontent.com/pod-product-compliance
Lightning Source LLC
Chambersburg PA
CBHW041526120626
46551CB00018B/2585